Coram Deo

Coram Deo

✦

Reflections on Presence

Kurtis S. Pearson, CFP®

iUniverse, Inc.
New York Lincoln Shanghai

Coram Deo
Reflections on Presence

iUniverse books may be ordered through booksellers or by contacting:

iUniverse
2021 Pine Lake Road, Suite 100
Lincoln, NE 68512
www.iuniverse.com
1-800-Authors (1-800-288-4677)

ISBN: 0-595-34834-3

Printed in the United States of America

Give me your lantern and compass, give me a map, So I can find my way to the sacred mountain, to the place of your presence….Psa 43

Contents

Introduction

✦

Coram Deo

This book title may bring an element of mystery or curiosity. That's good! We are going to ask that you look at your life in a new context. At the outset, we need to have you ponder this new concept. Can you really tell what's "real" and what's "fake" in your own life? Or have you even thought about the difference? You will in the pages that follow. It can't be avoided.

Have you ever been to a virtual reality theme park? I remember the raft ride. In a 10x12 room, you are placed on a raft with a big screen in front of you. The raft shifts, the tap water sprays and you could swear you were actually shooting the rapids.

It's all fake. They try to recreate the thrill without the risk. The attempt is to arrive at the adrenaline rush of living on the edge—but without any true danger!

In your own *real* life, have you ever felt absent while your life was happening? Have you ever wondered what it might feel like to be really alive? The danger with the adrenaline!

Imagine life with a strong sense of "presence" 24/7. All presence—all the time. A connection to the source of life with no degree of separation. There is a way that has Divine origins and leads us into being fully human.

The Protestant Reformation in the sixteenth century recovered many theological teachings that had been neglected by the medieval church. *Coram Deo* is one of those teachings. *Coram Deo* is a Latin phrase meaning: "before the face of God" or "in the presence of God." To stand *Coram Deo* is to be aware of God's presence and to be sensitive to the involvement of God in human life. To live

Coram Deo is to realize that God is ever working to forgive, heal, strengthen and save; it is to believe that God desires to be active in our lives and world.

This collection of essays is about recognizing and knowing that there is always something bigger going on in our lives than we can know or expect. It's also recognizing that we are connected to this Larger Life, whether we know it or not.

My own journey is littered with mountain peaks of presence and valleys of separation. I suspect you have too. Haven't you had those holy moments when you couldn't put words to the experience? And other times when you came away empty.

The truth is we face a dazzling daily array of distractions and temptations and interruptions leading us into a tangle of confusion and angst. The space between ourselves and our Father/Creator too often becomes blocked. Bombarded as we are by deadlines and projects and meetings and invitations and proposals, it's terribly difficult to remain *Coram Deo*. That's the challenge.

These separations lead us down the path of believing that we **are** the Large Life. By definition we become god in our life. A legend in our own mind. Fact is we were not created to be God; we were created to be human.

These writings are about informing and prodding us to presence—to *Coram Deo*. Being present with our life is to see the face of God. When that happens, we fully participate rather than sitting on the bench, hoping to get called into the game.

The saints of God are still those who live in that presence, in this life and in the life to come. They are a group of ordinary people—past, present and future—who have an extraordinarily close relationship with God. They are not perfectly sinless people, nor are they especially powerful people, but they are profoundly connected people—men and women who are linked directly to their own humanity and God. This makes them stand out in a world otherwise too well known for six or 60 or 600 degrees of separation.

Everyone's journey is different. Exploring our humanity and our connection to the "face of God" is an intensely individual adventure. This is not a self help book with 10 easy steps to gain control of your lives. The point is that we will never control our lives and that's a profoundly good thing.

In truth, the story of our lives is being written right in front of us. The story line is being revealed every day. Complete with a plot, main characters and an Author. These essays are a bit random and unpredictable, like life itself.

So, whether you choose to read them all in one sitting or you read them separately and perhaps return to them often, they are intended to help you recognize the signposts of your own personal life journey.

I am learning daily about standing squarely in the middle of my life and loving it there. This is not a place for the timid traveler. The virtual reality hype can't compare to the real deal.

Coram Deo is for those who have become weary of looking in a mirror and wondering who is really in the reflection. No spectators allowed; real life participants only. You will get wet and the raft will tip. In the turbulence and rapids, you will sense moments of danger, and pain, and then peace. The whitewater will subside. At that moment, you will find yourself present and participating in the life you were meant to live. From a sense of danger, you will feel the calm and the satisfaction of conquering and relish the promise of still waters.

Come be present with your life. The Large Life!

1

Life's Landscape

Open your eyes. What is the landscape stretching in front of you? From my rural retreat, I can stand on the front step and look to the East. What spreads before me is the rolling open landscape of central Iowa. It is open prairie down into the valley below, with a line of trees on the far horizon. This is where the sun comes from. This is where I have a clear view of deer in the meadow and wild turkeys like black dots in the distance. The red tail hawk soars with freedom and grace while on its mission.

The broad expanse of my life is open and spacious just like this view. There is much to look at and even more to see. A canvas with some basic parameters, but the details and the hues have yet to be chosen. There is a special beauty in this. It is calming and the canvas quietly waits for more work to be done. There is a rhythm to what is happening here. A place where time stands still but yet is also in a hurry to move on. Complete, yet unfinished.

I can walk around to my back deck, and I am immediately face-to-face with a mature timbered forest. Busy. Packed. And it has its own kind of activity. Squirrels, birds, foxes. Naked in the winter, and clothed with the mystery of leaves in the summer or subtle colors in the autumn. An active yellow-bellied sapsucker performs his own percussion on a hollow tree.

I can sit here for hours and find just as much beauty, in a different way. I can't see the sun set, but I can sense the creeping shadows, and know that another day is done. It is from here that I know I will hear the hoot owl and the whippoorwill. The timber holds a special mystery. It is from this view that I sense shadowy movement in the night. And I relish the surprises that can be mine for the listening and the seeing.

Showing up into your own life—*Coram Deo*—requires that you understand the landscape of your life. Three basic ideas to help us see and understand our own landscape. Past experience, family experience and created order.

Do you remember what was significant in your life twenty years ago? Most of what we struggled with then has long since been diminished in the wheel tracks of time. This is both good and bad. It's easy to get stuck on our past; this can be detrimental to our present and future. It is good to remember the lessons we learned and to record them for future reference.

JOURNALING

Writing about our experiences can be very therapeutic and helpful. Some need to write daily; others occasionally or monthly. The real benefit comes when you pull that twenty-year-old journal off the shelf and read about the struggles and triumphs of the past. Many emotions will bubble to the surface. This is good; this is human.

Journaling can help us realize repetitive trends to our lives. These are major clues to seeing the landscape for what it really is and living as a participant rather than a spectator.

FAMILY

Family is where it all started. The canvas was really blank before your Mom & Dad showed up. Then out of a moment of passion a genesis was formed, and it is you!

If we are really brave and courageous, we can go back to our families to listen and learn about our created identity. You know those stories your parents tell that have always been a little embarrassing. Listen to them in a new way next time. Ask this question—what is this life story telling me about myself?

The courage part is realizing that I am like many of my family members. Plotting out a time line of your life can be very instructive. Ask family members to help you. Talk about the significant events of your life and how they were handled.

The insight gained will begin to give you a perspective on the horizon and the tree line; the peaks and the valleys. *Coram Deo.* How can it really happen unless we embrace the ones who know us best?

CREATION

Of course this all happens in the context of Creation. Nature can teach us lessons that become parables of our own lives. Here's an example:

The Acorn Woodpeckers are interesting birds in the oak forest. Each fall they begin their annual routine. A local dead tree becomes their storage cabinet. They begin pecking storage holes in the dead tree, just large enough to hold an acorn. The stored acorns are available throughout the barren winter months for sustenance.

As the maturing acorns start falling to the ground, the woodpeckers begin, one at a time, picking them up and finding the proper storage hole. The acorns get pounded into the holes to withstand the wind, rain and snow.

Invariably, an acorn falls from its resting place and makes its way in the forest to a fertile spot. The acorn lies dormant until the warmth of the spring sun begins the thaw and the taproot begins to search for nutrients, sprouting an oak leaf and eventually growing into a sapling.

Studying the woodpecker alone is an amazing study in planning, preparation, instinct and nature in action. One could become enamored by the number of acorns stored per year per woodpecker. The travel patterns of the bird. The number of abandoned acorns each year. Graphs and charts could be built and predictions could be extrapolated for future trends. Some could even study the wind velocity and its impact on the food supply for Acorn Woodpeckers.

This micro approach has become a symbol of the trend of a life. Studying the woodpecker when we should be looking at the forest. Are you so busy stuffing acorns that you can't see the forest of your life?

There are happenings all around us that seem to scream importance. Upon further review and reflection, we get hints that there is much more going on than we realize at first glance. Something of real importance.

The woodpecker wept and wept and wept as the evening shadows stole.

For he had pecked and pecked and pecked all day on a concrete telegraph pole.

If the woodpecker had been listening, it would have moved on to a wood pole.

So, how would you sketch your own landscape? Use wide sweeping brush strokes to get you started. The detail work will come later. Leave enough space for the surprise and wonder of it all to be added later. There is a Master Artist who guides our hands along the way. These moments of surprise and wonder need a chapter of their own, Read on.

2

Wonder

There are few places where a sense of surprise, wonder and awe are on display. The Wild is one of those places. In the middle of a forest there are surprises too numerous to mention. Put me to the test. I dare you to go sit in a forest or wild prairie for two whole hours. No books, no MP3 players, just you and nature. You will not be disappointed.

One of my favorite stories is from John Muir's collection. John was a naturalist and avid explorer. He was also an excellent writer. He was able to put words to some of the glorious adventures of his life. He entered creation with the innocence of a child and the reverence of a friar.

<u>Account from The Wilderness World of John Muir</u>

[Edwin Way Teale/Houghton-Mifflin, circa 1954]

In 1874 (Muir) was visiting a friend in the Sierra Mountains. This friend had a cabin near a tributary of the Yuba River. It was perfect. John could go exploring and return to the cabin for a respite.

One December day, a storm came in from the Pacific. It was a fierce storm, bending the junipers toward the ground. Can't you see John snug in the cabin, next to the fire protected from the harsh elements? Muir was made of something different. He did throw another log on the fire, then bravely strode out of the cabin to enjoy the storm. He climbed a high ridge, found the tallest Douglas fir and climbed to the top. That is where he held on for dear life, riding out the storm.

This is embracing wonder. Naming it, claiming it and entering into it. It is a place for the brave, because it will mean that you figuratively go out in the storm and climb the fir to hold on for dear life. This is *Coram Deo*!

I have my own version of a similar experience. It isn't quite as dramatic, but for me it was a moment of surprise and wonder.

I have grown into the habit of Sunday sabbaticals. Taking a break from the noise and demands of a rich life and simply reflecting. Meditation is a place to digest all that life has been feeding you.

Last December, I headed out for some meditation to a special forest. For the previous three weeks I had been out to a wilderness area and seen deer every time. Watching deer is fascinating to say the least. They are nervous and shifty, but also elegant and graceful. This particular week happened to be the first week of deer season and I knew the dynamics of the day were going to be different. I also somewhat expected the deer to be in deeper cover, escaping the hunters. They seem to know.

I arrived at my usual post overlooking a deep ravine. It was taking a little extra time to unwind. The week had been hectic and I was recounting and reliving the work and family situations. I started to look for deer, openly admitting that my expectations were coming true—the deer had headed for deeper cover.

After awhile, silence purges the mind, allowing us to enter a different, slower space in time. The quiet was scrubbing my mind clean from the demands of life and I was beginning to enter the rhythm of the wild. Then I began to see them.

A young buck was scraping the snow and frost to find the treasured acorn. A doe was close by and then there were a couple other yearlings walking through. The surroundings were coming alive. The deer had been there all along. I was the one who had changed. There is an adventuresome world coming alive around me; I was finally ready to listen and participate.

Do you want to cultivate some wonder in your life? There really isn't a 10-step list, however there are a few techniques to incorporate into your lifestyle.

Start building some "margin" into your lives. Think of how this book is constructed. The margins are deliberate. The words don't go all the way to the edges of the page. They leave some open space left and right to let you focus and be comfortable. The same with the "rest stop" each paragraph provides to let you catch your breath and prepare for a new thought. A sense of margin is missing in too many lives. You can change that.

I'm convinced there is a binding relationship between wonder and listening. Listening has become such a rare occurrence in our lives. Wonder is diminished when our lives are full of talking and noise. Perhaps the greatest sound of all is no sound at all. Begin today to build enough "margin" into your life to really listen. You will hear things you never heard before.

The power of observation is also important. Look around. Find ways to put your own circumstances in context. I remember many shopping trips as a young child, where we would sit at the front of the store and wait for our grandfather to pick us up. I watched the people. A mother struggling with her children; the rambunctious youth showing too little consideration for others; the elderly exerting extra effort to go about their daily chores. The happiness or sadness on people's faces. They all told a story. Through observation, it helps us frame our own behavior and code for the way we lead our lives and the choices we make. Observation can be very formative.

Children provide tremendous inspiration. They are mostly margin. They have an unlimited sense of wonder and exploration. They want to touch and taste everything! They run without fear of falling. They shout. They experiment. They find special joy in playing in the rain and the mud, while parents fret about them "catching cold" and "getting dirt on the rug." They play with all-out effort, and sleep with an uncluttered mind.

As grown ups, the sense of wonder is something we learn to put on a shelf. The business world can't accept wonder as a viable response. We have to be about facts and figures or we will get laughed out of the boardroom. Wonder gets choked to death, and we are all the murderer.

We would do well to start hanging with kids more often. Watch them at play. Kids have a special gift of exploring the wonder all around them. To them it is a new and unfettered drive to learn and to appreciate. Yes, they play with an unbounded joy. But they can also show us the way to gain new insight without all of the adult limitations.

Creation is full of wonder. There have been so many times that a walk in the woods has surprised me. An unexpected great horned owl that I watched for a good while. A squirrel attacking the hickory nuts. They can really jump! The greatest part of a walk in the woods is when you stand still and focus.

A final tip is the significance of silence and solitude. Solitude is a bit of a misnomer. We really need to be alone with ourselves. Truth borne out of personal experience is the best kind of truth. When the noise is gone, we are able to hear reality without bias.

Spirits are restored and hope is renewed through shutting up and getting away. We are also brought in front of our wounds. Every human heart has wounds and pain that have to be embraced as the path to pure joy. Joy is borne of sorrow and there is no sorrow greater than the wounds in our heart. Choosing to ignore such hurt may lead to an occasional dose of happiness, manufactured wonder and emptiness. But that is temporary and very unfulfilling. There is nothing as empty as wonder and awe that has its source in illusion or entertainment.

Conversely, there is great wonder to behold when you hear it with new ears and see it with new eyes and embrace it with a new heart. When you invest time in places of wonder, you will come away with your own John Muir story. Live on the edge of wonder. You'll love it.

3

Name

I remember vividly a recent social gathering. Invariably the obvious question comes up—"So, what do you do?" As soon as I answer that question the conversationalist will make assumptions about who I am. That may be unfortunate, but it's the way we work.

How did you get your name? As you may have noticed by now, my name is spelled with a "K". My initials are KSP. My Father's initials are CSP. My parents wanted our initials to be different, hence Kurt with a "K".

Some of you have good family friends that are your namesake. Others were named after a movie star or cultural icon. Our names impact our identity. The way we perceive our identity shapes the way we look at life and our lives. So, who are you? When you think of descriptive words to define yourself, how would you begin?

To many institutions we are a number. That makes a statement. The culture is tilted to making us into functions or at best, a demographic that acts a certain way when confronted with an image or situation. Narrowing humanity to a predictable task or behavior set is rampant in our worlds.

As you might guess, I take issue with this. Our names should not be reduced to a number. Sure it might be convenient, but as this happens all around it has impact on the very places where we have to maintain our sense of person—the family and the church.

These places ought to be about leading us into spacious names for ourselves that teach and instruct us about the mystery of person, the holiness of being created and the roles of life that are large and unique to our humanity.

Our language struggles with words to describe the mystery of humanity. Most adjectives should add to the mystery and give it room, rather than narrowing the definition of our person.

One narrow example is how our culture wants to name us sexually. Sexual identity is a broad, holy mystery. The descriptor "lady" immediately communicates mystery. Our consumeristic culture leads us down to a definition of ladies that has its source based on what men think. As a lady you will be sexy if you have the correct nail polish, hair color and wardrobe configuration. Ladies are much more attractive to men when they are in touch with their created identity, rather than their consumerized image. These tricks only narrow our definition and forces all of us into a box, herded like a bunch of cattle. Such narrowing can only lead to shallowness and a sense of being unfulfilled. It is not a pathway to inner peace.

Lets take a peek at some of those spacious names that are so large they almost entice us into Living Large.

PILGRIM

What comes to your mind? Thanksgiving? The original settlers in our country? In elementary school we recreated the first Thanksgiving feast. The teachers needed a black cast iron pot to put over the fire for beef stew. We had one in our family—with one caveat—it had been used as a planter for flowers. I remember scrubbing and scrubbing before it could also become a cooking vessel. The stew was decent, with a somewhat earthy taste!

When John Wayne referred to someone as "Pilgrim" he rolled it off his tongue in such a way it became part of his movie persona. But Pilgrim had a significant definition that pre-dated Thanksgiving or the Duke. One of the best images of this word is the pilgrimage Israelites made several times a year up to Jerusalem for feasts and parties. Their story is full of pilgrim vernacular and experience. Somewhat of a mirror for all of our lives. Wilderness, exodus, salvation, wars, miracles, dysfunctional families (re-read Genesis 37).

A true pilgrim is on a journey. Watching and waiting for the next step. Looking forward to the Promised Land. Usually on a path with some comrades. Do you see yourself as a Pilgrim? What does your wilderness journey look like?

FATHER

We all have one. Our thoughts on Father go the full range of human emotion. Just linger over the name. Think about your own. Think about a priest. Why are they called Fathers?

This is intended to be one of the most intimate naming words we have. One of the ideas is that we were given in a family. The family is the place where, for good or bad, we first learn our names. Oh yes, you are a Clancy.....or oh, you are a Clancy? Our Fathers have had much to do with how we became comfortable in our own name.

What is the story of your Father? Most of us wrestle all our lives with Father. Either the Father we have here, the Father over there, or some of us have the privilege of being Father. You will Live Larger if you go there and develop a sense of well being. One of the best stories of Father is included in the parable of the Lost Son [Luke 15: 11-32].

Henri Nouwen, one of my favorite authors, wrote an entire book on the Lost Son Story. One of his observations is that at various times in life, we are the Father from the story. We offer grace and mercy. Other times, we are the repentant son, begging for grace and mercy. Yet other times, we are the older son, rebelling against grace and mercy.

All earthly Fathers also pass wounds to their children. No one is exempt. It's nothing to ignore or become hateful about; it's something to embrace and forgive. Despite our best efforts as Fathers, we are human. We should learn very quickly that one of the best places for a spacious view of our life is to go back to where it began.

STEWARD

Perhaps you remember the scene in the movie *Rudy*. Rudy's dream is to play football at Notre Dame. His first hurdle is to get the grades to make it into the revered University. After several quarters at a community college, he finds Notre Dame has turned him down several times. Now he is waiting every day for the letter once again. He goes to church and asks a very wise priest to pull some strings for him. The Priest's response, "Son, I have learned after 30 years in the ministry two very important truths. 1. There is a God. 2. I am not Him."

Our role and name is to Steward or manage. Not to own. Owners have rights. Stewards have responsibilities. What do we have to Steward? Time, Talent, Money are three of the basic resources. Time and money are quantifiable and would have the appearance of control, but we can't really stop time or start it, which means we have no control. We can't really know how much money we will have flowing in at any point in time, or when it will dissipate. No control. Talents—that's an open book. The way we broaden our talents has a lot to say about our identity. Something you do control.

CHILD

You probably have some young children around—your own or perhaps grandchildren. Observe them sometime. The wonder, innocence, honesty and curiosity are examples of life. How do we stay young and dependent on Father?

Pride and arrogance are surefire ways to reduce the mystery of life. Business owners are taught to become self-reliant. This may be rewarded in the business world, but in life it is a recipe for failure and emptiness.

It is an endearing title to think of yourself as a child. A son or daughter of the most high Father. This puts us on a path of exploration and adventure. Digging into this title leads to a path that we just can't get on if we are thinking we are a President or CEO.

Have you ever noticed how kids are always looking up for direction or help. Not a bad picture at all. It sure allows for some relaxation rather than having to perform up to a standard.

Those who accept these truths live large, spacious lives. It takes the pressure off. We are not good at playing God; we need to keep getting better at being human.

Any descriptive word we use to define the mystery of our person is going to fall short. It's still good to go there and think about the words you are using to describe yourself.

One warning: be careful about using names or labels that are all about functions. It's so easy to become defined by a particular activity rather than who we really are. This happens all the time in the business world. Job descriptions are designed to erase the mystery of person and define tasks as responsibilities. These can be useful, but they can't begin to define us in our away-from-work lives.

If we allow functions and "doing" to define who we are, we will feel used and abused. Some in business will switch to a different company, hoping things are different there. They won't be. By definition, business has to be about quantifiable results; no mystery allowed. Business is about "doing", not "being."

Religion in North America is operating much the same way. Results are measured by attendance, offerings, programs offered and souls rescued. Program directors, even if volunteers, are defined by a function by the church leadership. Dehumanizing the parishioner in the name of a Higher power.

What if in social settings we respond to the question "What do you do?" by replying "I live to serve others." Would this be closer to the truth than identifying your employer? It should be.

We need to live large in the identity we were created into. And to the identity we refine for ourselves. This is a wide mystery that is still being written into the story of your life and mine. In this sense, we get to name ourselves. Pilgrim. Father. Steward. Child. All of the above.

4

Senses

o o o o o o o o o o o o o o o o o o o o o o o o o o o o o o o o o

"O, taste and see that the Lord is good; blessed is the man that trusts in him."

—*Psalms 34:8*

Our senses offer incredible clues to living *Coram Deo*. Presence with your own life has to include the body and the way we are made. The way we inhale truth and exhale creation.

We are sensual. The taste and touch of living is an incredible way to adore creation. Remember the last meal you ate that had several unique tastes? A grilled steak that has been rubbed with special spices, topped with a bleu cheese sauce. Serve it up with a baked potato, butter, sour cream and full bodied merlot. Wow! Aren't your taste buds doing somersaults? Aren't you ready to put some flavor in your life?

A good meal is a work of art; a place in time to admire and adore. Typically a good meal is accompanied with fellowship, introducing looking, listening and talking. Some of the best meals I have experienced have had surprises in conversation, compounding the mystery and enjoyment of the moment.

Our sensuality is a beautiful piece of creation and can be used for great good. The opposite is also true. Let's look at a couple of evil tendencies and a couple of positive ones.

One evil default tendency we have is to use our senses for comparison. We forget that we are made with incredible capacity to create. There is a default track in us that shelves our one-of-a-kind giftedness for the sin of covetousness. The kind way to say this is our tendency to live life by comparisons.

We compare ourselves to our neighbors, our friends, our enemies and practically anyone who crosses our path. But, as soon as we begin to compare, we are using others rather than honoring them. This is a dead end street that either leaves us feeling defeated because we don't measure up, or foolishly proud because we do. Meanwhile we are separated from *Coram Deo* because the focus is not on listening to our own lives, but extrapolating it through the lives of others.

Doing so kills our sensuality.

Another separation from proper sensory application occurs when we use things to satisfy the eternal longing in our souls. Ours is a lonely culture. Everyone I know is aching for something meaningful. The marketing departments know this and create all types of products to try to fill the void.

This is where free enterprise and spirituality bed down and create all kinds of little consumerisms. The most dangerous form this takes is religious consumerism. We begin to believe we are using the senses for something good, but in fact the underlying goal is to be self-serving and self-righteous.

One of the ways our senses were meant to be used is in worship and adoration. We were created to worship. But many times the worship is misplaced. Every fall there are nine Sundays when more than 70,000 zealots gather to cheer on the Kansas City Chiefs in Arrowhead Stadium. I have attended many of these worship services and promoters know how to entice every sense into the event. And, if it's Monday Night, they kick it up a notch!

There are also the Sabbath experiences in a more subtle setting—a forest. At times I have stopped to smell the earth in the middle of the Midwestern prairie. The wary doe or the ghostly hoot owl capture the imagination and captivate eyesight. The heightened awareness makes one come alive and wonder at what will happen next. For my money, no last-minute touchdown can compare!

Anther positive use of the senses is to adore or show honor to another. Encouragement. Writing a note, making a phone call, walking a pie to a neighbor or listening to a friend in need are all good examples. Your day is richer, and so is the recipient of such kindnesses.

Before we can really nourish another, we have to start inside our own self. Isn't it interesting that one of the best ways we can overcome an anxiety attack is to firmly plant our feet and begin massaging our legs and arms. This has a nourishing effect on us.

To be effective with others we have to learn to use of our senses to inhale the truth about who we are, who we are not and what we are going to do about it, if anything. A good yell, or sob, can play a vital role in nourishing a healthy soul.

Of course the most interesting thought related to sense is the fact that God almighty describes himself with senses. Jesus, being God, took on the senses as part of his humanity.

For now, we live in this skin and wonder at these marvelous senses we have been given to experience the created order around us.

Pardon me. I smell the grill; better grab that steak.

Six Senses

Listen!

He comes in the rustling and the giggles.

The crying and the barking.

Background sounds carry the depth.

Leading us into the rhythm of repentance.

Taste!

Taking Him inside by chew and swallow.

Participating at internalizing the mystery.

Physical eats; spiritual nourishment.

Daily Bread, not yesterday or tomorrow, just today.

Look!

Eyes—the window to the soul.

Gatekeepers of the night watch.

Most are looking, but never see.

Observe the beauty; don't blink.

Smell!

Fragrance divine wafting through time.

Intense and personal—taking us to a space.

Memories refreshed by the odor of the moment.

Seasons of smell for a new time of space.

Touch!

Practical outworking of the heart.

Good work with hands and feet that declare.

God is alive and at work today and always.

Smooth and rough—the texture of the artist.

Speak!

Words can kill or give life.

Tongues are swords or salve.

Healing or hurting syllables.

Silence speaks high volume.

5

Living in Skin

Several years ago the famous professional golfer Payne Stewart tragically died in a private plane crash, some 42,000 feet closer to Heaven. The memorial service had many public figures sharing thoughts and eulogies. One of his friends commented that Payne "had recently become very comfortable in his own skin."

There have been many times in my own life that I have wanted to run from what I was at the time. Regrettably, I wasn't present with my life and what it was becoming. *Coram Deo* has to mean a comfort level with self.

This doesn't start with skin (the external), it has to start with the Father of Ages. Before we got skin, we met with Father. Father created in our spirits a special set of gifts to remind us of our connection with Him.

The journey in skin begins with stones littering the path back home. Crumbs get eaten by others or the Evil One; we've got to be alert for the stone signposts. You remember the familiar childhood story:

Hansel was a bright kid. He couldn't help it if his family was so poor they could not support their children. He had secretly vowed that his life would not end up like theirs. But he had no idea what lay in store.

In the famous Grimms' Fairy Tale, Hansel and Gretel were cast out by their struggling family. Forced to fend for themselves in the deep, dark woods. There was no hope for safe return. But Hansel was resourceful and wise beyond his years. Being forewarned that he and his sister were to be exiled from their home by their destitute parents, he was thoughtful enough, even as a child, to secret some shining pebbles from their homestead into his pocket for their unanticipated journey of fear and despair.

He also looked back from time to time so he would recognize the trail they had followed and perhaps recollect some landmarks they had passed if they ever had to retrace their steps. An occasional stone dropped along the way would lead them back to safe passage, if the time should come. And the thought gave him comfort as they penetrated deeper into the foreboding forest.

He had planned ahead. They would be safe, even in the most threatening of times. The stones would lead them home. And so they did. In time, he and Gretel would return safely to their home, much to the relief of their parents who had sentenced them to a life on their own in a distant land. And, the father was overjoyed with their return.

But again the parents reached a moment in their lives when the children were cast aside a second time, and driven deep into the woods, expecting never to return again. This time, Hansel had no pebbles. Fortified only with a tiny loaf of bread for himself and another for his sister, he faced dread and uncertainty and rejection. Looking back was not going to be enough.

But the children devised a plan. He and Gretel would have to survive somehow by her sacrificing what little bread she had with her brother so he could shred his own loaf into small pieces and use them for trail markers. Somehow, they would survive. His tiny trail of bread crumbs was all he could count on to perhaps provide a second safe passage.

But Hansel's plan proved flawed. As he dribbled his few crumbs along the way, the innocent children were being followed every step of their journey by greedy birds, who silently swooped down on their trail and devoured the crumbs. Hansel's escape plan had been compromised. And, as they tried once again to return, they found themselves hopelessly lost. Familiar landmarks were not enough. And they appeared doomed. They counted on no second chances.

Around the bend, in the disguise of a helpful stranger, they were befriended by a kindly old lady who offered them food and shelter and comfort. They felt cheered by her apparent kindness and they accepted her charm and hospitality with relief. But, instead they fell into her trap. Hansel was imprisoned, and Gretel was enslaved into servitude for the devious woman of the woods. It was only through Gretel's ingenuity, when asked to climb into a raging oven fire, that the woman was instead devoured by her own flame, and the siblings were able to make a hasty retreat. Lost, but free!

In their freedom, they looked at their surroundings in a totally new way. The forest was not as scary as before. They started hearing the beauty of the wind in the boughs. They listened with delight to the songbirds and admired their care-free behavior in flight. They heard the rush of a babbling brook with its symphony of musical tones. They marveled at the artistry of colorful flowers on the forest floor. And they found a new direction. It was the songbirds and the soothing rivers that led them home, with a new appreciation for the forest. It was their friend, now, not their enemy.

Again, a grieving father was there to welcome them home with a warm embrace. And this time, they rejoiced, and remained in the loving arms of the father. They were safely home, to stay.

What does the journey look like as you stumble forward and embrace the "stones" on life's path? These holy moments can't really be described by words.

There are descriptions for the result of someone living in *Coram Deo*. Try these on:

"He's comfortable in his own skin"

"She just has this way about her; she really understands."

"Everything she touches turns to gold."

"He marches to the beat of a different drummer."

"Her elevator doesn't go all the way to the top."

"They are very eccentric."

We have all known people that could be described with these statements. Beginning to understand the journey to home, will lead us down a counter-culture path that will be noticed and we may find ourselves ostracized and alone. So be it.

Being lonely is a great place to be as long as you are free. Pursuing the path of the Spirit is as free as we can be standing in our temporary earthly home.

For now, *Coram Deo* may be bound by the limitations of time, space and skin. These barriers can easily become the focus, but they were never intended to be. Before we know it, we are ensnared in a small life by the "devious woman in the woods."

Once these self-imposed barriers burn in flames, we see life in a whole new way. We hear the birds chirping and we hear the brook. Those who work in hospice will speak of the connection that the dying ones have with creation. The skin is fading and once and for all they will be free from the barriers. Eternally free.

My guess is that something like this happened to Payne Stewart. Perhaps he stopped seeing himself as a great golfer and started seeing himself as a child of the Father. Go and do likewise while there is still time.

6

Centering Your Life

o o o o o o o o o o o o o o o o o o o o o o o o o o o o o o o o

"Walk worthy of the calling…"

—Ephesians 4:1

Life requires that we attempt to find balance between "being" and "doing"—a daunting task, to be sure. How can we answer Paul's encouragement to the Ephesians to 'walk worthy of the calling'?

My challenge, and yours, is to want to get out there and walk—better yet run—on the road God called you to travel. There is no time for sitting on your hands. And there certainly is no excuse for strolling off onto a pathway that leads nowhere. It is imperative that this walk through life be done with humility and discipline—not in fits and starts. The walk needs to be deliberate and with purpose, pouring ourselves out for others in acts of love and kindness, while staying alert to notice differences and to quickly mend broken fences. Leave nothing unattended.

If life is lived in a constant spin cycle, we can run the risk of either spinning out of control, or at least wobbling from an absence of balance in the multiple facets of our complicated lives.

Picture a set of old fashion scales, with its two pans balanced in the center by a fulcrum pivot point. Weight placed in one pan, will have an impact on the other pan, creating an imbalance.

This is such a good picture of how we make life decisions each day. Usually we are only capable of comparing two categories of our life at one time. Put career in

27

one pan; put family in the other. Insert a daughter playing basketball at 3:30pm. Going to the game will cut the work day short, creating potential guilt. Working a full day will lead to guilt about missing the game. And so it goes. Living with the scales and balancing our lives is a difficult and perhaps impossible proposition.

Even if we learn to manage the guilt in comparing two areas of our lives, we haven't even added all the other categories to the scales. After a while, we have to admit we are out of balance.

Is there another way? There has to be. Whenever we are constantly setting ourselves up for failure, there has to be a better way to do things.

Let's shift the focus from the pans to the fulcrum. Change terminology from balance to centered. Coming to the fulcrum and examining the basics of life are the first courageous steps leading us down a path of freedom and peace.

Investing time at the "center" means you acknowledge several things:

1. I'm incapable of balancing my life. In other words, loading up the pans and keeping them level is not my job.

2. Decisions that inflict guilt need to be examined more closely. Create some space and time to think about the feelings surrounding certain decisions. You will begin to get clarity as time passes.

3. Time is limited and it's the most valuable asset we have. We do not control our time—we steward it. Allocating certain blocks of time to each category of our life works well until something unplanned comes up. Then what do we do? Time controls us and the best we can do is make general choices as stewards. *Life is what happens while we are making up our minds.*

4. Time gains significance when we escape it. This is a key to being centered rather than balanced. When was the last time you were able to be somewhere with no regard for a clock? This frees us to begin making decisions.

Our western world view tends to be very linear. We have priorities and here is the list. We will spend more time on priority 1 than on priority 2. If we don't, then we are imbalanced. Unfortunately, this thinking will inevitably lead to incredible frustration and boredom. Where is the space in life for the unexpected and the mystery? Frankly, reducing life to a list turns out to be a small way to live. The sooner we accept this prospect, the better. This lesson is best learned at 30 rather than 60.

The more promising alternative is to adopt and embrace a journey and adventure mentality. Wake up every morning wondering what bend will the road take today? How will I react to it? Will I even see it, or miss it totally?

There is more going on than shifting some time from one side of the scales to the other side. Understand that the shifts at the "pan level" are not actually in our control.

What we are really talking about is the tension between "Being" and "Doing". It's easy to think that these two are mutually exclusive. When I'm off "finding myself"(being), the "Doing" in life begins to take shape. When I'm out doing, it begins to shed light on the mystery of giftedness and talents.

These two ideas are interrelated and we need *both* to really explore the adventure in life. This is an activity to help us at the center of the scales. Rather than allotting a certain amount of time for God, at the "pan level" in our priority list, we begin to see a spiritual connection in everything we do. All time becomes holy, not just when we are engaged in religious activity. The time invested to clean the toilets is just as holy as the time invested listening to a sermon. I know this requires a huge leap of faith to re-order our lives in this manner.

The noble idea of trying to live a "centered life" is often a matter of perception. Living at the "pan level" carries perceptions related to others. Many times our linear priority list doesn't really reflect our priorities. Those are imposed on us by the perceptions of others. How easy is it for you to say "no"? Centered individuals know and understand the Calling of their lives and they can't afford to deviate from the path of the journey.

Linear priority-based lives are always busy with activities that get crowded into our lives by others. When we allow that to happen, we never really know why we are doing something—we just are. It is even difficult to rearrange our schedules at the basic level because of what others would think. This is no way to live. In fact,

I'll take it one step further. You are dying if you are living this way—both physically and emotionally.

Living the adventure from the Center of who you are will look very strange to those around you. You will pursue activities that will be unique and leave others scratching their heads in wonder at when you became so weird. This is what makes us so alive! There is a sense of calm and peace that we just can't get to in the linear lifestyle.

How do you get there? Well true to the western mind, you want a list and a detailed map, right? The best I can do is provide a few clues.

1.   Which of your current life activities makes you feel more alive? Invest more time there.

2.   Ask some who love you most what you are good at doing. Do you agree with them?

3.   Who do you know that is Centered; go see them.

4.   Enter solitude; listen in silence. The Center will find you if you seek it.

7

Reality vs. Expectations

The winter sun was barely up. It was early, cold and down right miserable. Add the wind chill and it had to be twenty below. Still, maybe today was the day. This might be the moment when I beat the wild and finally reached what I was striving for. Great things could happen in this hostile environment. I would have crossed my fingers if they hadn't been frozen stiff.

Odd how the seasons penetrate our body and our soul. My quest had begun months ago, in the searing heat of summer. As hot then as it was cold now. In those hot, sticky days of summer, I got the books that would drive my imagination. With boyish enthusiasm, suddenly I was going to be a fur trapper. I had ventured into our timber often enough to know that the woodlands surrounding our farm held incredible potential for harvesting some furs. I discounted the possums and the skunks and focused on more valuable game. Raccoons, fox, badger—and even beaver! It was going to be a great adventure, measured by my soaring expectations.

That was summer. Now, 6 months later, the expectations and hopes from the dog days of summer seemed like a remote memory. Checking the trap line before school in sub zero hadn't really crossed my mind back in July. Not to mention, my efforts weren't meeting with the success that I had read about. I knew that my luck was about to change. It had to. Reality was starting to dash my expectations. That just couldn't happen.

But the hard truth was that the bitterness of winter had cooled my ambition. My trap line had slowly shrunk amid the rigorous Iowa winter. This morning there were three traps to check and I couldn't wait to be finished. The first two traps were barren. As usual. The three-wheeler droned on as tears from the cold streamed down my face. A mile and a half to the third trap. I crossed the ravine and came into the clearing, and came face-to-face with mean. Teeth barred, growls and ugly. I was hoping the chain on the trap would continue to hold. I did then what every brave fifteen year old adolescent male would do…headed home to get Dad!

"Dad, you won't believe it, I caught a wolf or a grey fox. Can you help me?"

"Sure, let's go" Dad said.

When we got to the third trap, I was so proud…already thinking about how I was going to write an article detailing my great capture and send it in to *Fur-Fish-Game* magazine. Then came those words that crushed my career as a trapper.

"It's just a dog," my Dad said disgustedly.

The next several minutes have been erased from my mind due to the overwhelming sense of failure. I know we got the dog out of the trap.

The disappointment and failure was sure different than the stories I had read about in the magazines. That was an important life lesson, though. Seldom do expectations and reality cross paths at the moment you want them to.

Let's move forward to several years to the setting of my financial practice. There are many stories of those who are ready to quit working mentally, emotionally and physically, but financially they can't. When that reality sets in, their expectations are shattered. Shattered expectation leads to disappointment. If disappointment is not grieved properly, it moves up the ladder to anger and rage.

We all have needs. With those needs come expectations that those needs will be met somehow, leading to incredible hope. These expectations can easily become much larger than our needs. They build over time and can enlarge big like a balloon, expanding our hope to Pollyanna proportions. Eventually a large dose of reality comes in the form of a needle and pops the balloon, shattering all hope.

Opal was a lady in her early 60's when we first met. She wanted help applying for the benefit from a life insurance policy. I will never forget our interaction. These were her comments to me, "Kurt, my husband and I were married for 40 years. I helped put him through medical school and he became a very fine physician. As most doctors, his schedule became hectic, crowding out time for family and other activities. His standard line for this was, 'Someday we will take the money we've been saving, retire and really enjoy life'. Well, three years ago he was diagnosed with cancer and now he's gone. Now what? I can't imagine going on, and all this money means nothing without him. We were going to travel and see places. Now I'm all alone and he's gone."

Coram Deo is about knowing that our reality of daily life is matching up with how we are supposed to be living. A sense of inner contentment and peace that we are following the path we were created to follow.

The expectations or dreams we all have may not come to pass. When that happens it is vital that we grieve the loss. The good news is that sorrow and sadness are the seedbeds for hope and true joy.

If we choose not to grieve, we will become angry and bitter. This is no way to live. We check out on our life and become a spectator. We have built a blockade on the path and we can't get around it. The anger and depression rob us of any joy in the present day.

These wounds have to be healed through grief before we can live *Coram Deo*. Many of us will need a guide to take us into these wounds for healing. Over the years, we have built up the blockade and it's so large and strong, we have the perception that we can't bust through it. In reality it is made of crepe paper and with the right touch, we discover that and bust into the sunshine on the other side.

It takes much courage to live this way. I have traveled this path and do work daily to make sure that blockades don't turn into fortresses. I want to encourage you to do the same.

Everyone's path into their wounds will take a different path, but there may be a few common characteristics:

1. Anytime you get angry, you have to know that there is a root cause. The root may have nothing to do with the anger of the moment.

2. Learn to put words to the sorrow and loss you have had in life. Getting the words out into the open allows them space to live or die as a reality.

This can be done through writing or speaking. Sometimes no one else will see or hear this but you.

3. Emotional reactions become signposts along the path. Listen intently to these reactions. I recently got emotional during a certain scene in a movie. It didn't seem that anyone else in the theater had the same reaction I did. There is something in that reaction that will show me more about myself. *Coram Deo*.

4. Look for a guide. Search for someone who has learned how to do this in his own life. Someone that is ahead of you in the journey and can help you untangle yourself from yourself.

God speed as you dig into the wounds and allow the flashlight to illuminate the corners of your heart. This is *Coram Deo*. Living in the present with an eye on the future!

8

Learning to Lament

He didn't know what to do next. She wanted him to leave, but where could he go that was safe? It's quite a thing at 48 to take a snapshot of your life and realize you don't have anything. No safe places; no one that would really miss you if you were gone. At another time, it would have driven him to the bottle. Not now—he was even past that.

Despair is a terrible thing, as bad as it gets and worse. Then little Jackie and young Jack crossed his mind. His wife loved those kids; he did too—as much as a desperate person can really love someone. Suddenly, he got so mad that he was ready to do something drastic. He could never hurt them, but he could hurt himself. Yeah, that would show them. That would show them what they were doing to him.

No, that was the exact self-centered attitude that was the source of his problems. Just have to live with the despair, he thought.

To pass the time he went for a drive. He remembered the way his father used to treat him as a teenager. One night he came home late and his father woke up and beat him with a belt. This wasn't the first time, nor would it be the last. But it was a definable moment because he determined as soon as he could he would escape his home and never come back.

He often wondered what it looked like to be Father to his own kids. He found himself falling into the same patterns of anger and hatred. The only thing that has kept him from beating on them was his strong determination that he would not become his father.

The realization is flooding him that he is his father. A new wave of despair and hopelessness sweeps his being.

How low can a soul go before it hits the point of no return? Why? The ache of his heart had been festering for years and the attempts to find meaning and purpose from everyone and everything had continued his spiral. He drove out past the country church where they had been married. He remembered the expectations he had. Finally someone who really loves me and someone I can love. Reciting some vows doesn't make someone a lover anymore than a shower makes someone a swimmer. 'Til death we part'…there's that idea again.

His mind drifted to the office as he continued to drive. Now that was a bright spot. Performing for a paycheck brought a sense of security. It was defined and easy. At least for a while. Recently he had noticed that he couldn't wait for the weekends, to be done with the treadmill of chasing dollars for a couple days. During the weekends, he couldn't wait to get back to work. How long had he been living this way? Far too long. Now what?

They will never know if it was him that crossed the center line or the other car. Our desperate friend passed from this life—already dead.

The aches of our heart cannot be ignored, for they are the path to incredible peace and joy. Our choice is whether we will embrace them or run. Being present with life has to include the sorrow. *Coram Deo.*

> *When life is heavy and hard to take, go off by yourself. Enter the silence. Bow in prayer. Don't ask questions: Wait for hope to appear. Don't run from trouble. Take it full face, the "worst" is never the worst.*
>
> —[Lamentations 3]

What do you do with despair and anguish? In America we are conditioned to handle pleasure, profits, and peace. It comes somewhat natural, playing into our natural human tendency toward self-gratification. Writhing in the pit of hell isn't a focus in our families or our neighborhoods. There is really only one response—learn to grieve and lament.

Grief is going to be a very popular topic over the next 30 years as the Baby Boomers continue to bury their parents and begin to pass themselves. Many will struggle to handle the pain. The focus will be the typical self-help approach used in America—let's fix it. There is a different way that fosters true healing from the inside to the outside.

At the risk of sounding glib, we have to embrace the pain and enter into it. Several other cultures have given us clues.

SACKCLOTH AND ASHES

Remember the ancient story of Job. He lost everything and sat in sackcloth and ashes.

A well-known family in our community just lost their wife and mother at 53 years. Rumor has it that the husband is taking it hard. What if he discontinued work indefinitely and sat in the front yard with a fire going in sweat pants and a t-shirt? Taking ashes from the fire and rubbing them into his clothing. What would this really accomplish? Wouldn't she want him to "get on with his life?" Really. How can you get on with life when you have had to stare down death?

The pain of loss has to have space to be processed. Read the wisdom again from the ancient writings of King Solomon. *"Wait in the silence.....don't ask questions.....wait for hope to appear..."*

In our culture, after a short week off work, he will go back to the office, burying his pain in the drugs of choice—busyness, denial, medications or alcohol, etc.

LAMENT

Others will try to reach out. "How are you doing?" Some will really mean it; others don't really want to know, they are just asking out of courtesy. It would be great if he answered honestly. Lashing out with some true laments are a critical part of the healing process.

Some need to write those laments; others need to speak them. Regardless, they need to come out in full force. We are not good at this. Trust me. God and the people who really love us can handle it. Telling someone off is very therapeutic! Try it sometime in the proper setting.

By the way, the proper setting for this would be a family or a church. Wouldn't it be great to walk into church some Sunday and observe a guy in the foyer cussing God out. "What happened to him?" "Oh his Mom died this past week and he's pissed."

Our religious leaders could really do some good over the next three decades by teaching us how to lament.

So, when the pain becomes unbearable, create space in your life to let it teach you. There is much to learn from pain. Enter the silence. Bow in prayer. Don't ask questions. Wait for hope to appear.

Learn the language of pain. A good lament is invaluable first step to healing.

Grieving isn't a 10-step process. It is a place of loneliness where we really learn to be with self and wait. We are out of control and it's all right. Grieving doesn't have to be about the loss of life. It can be about the loss of a job, retiring, a child that is leaving, or maybe a frightening health issue. We have to reach an acceptance of all that's wrong and make an admission that we are powerless in the face of it all.

I'm running into the danger of adding to the problem by continuing to add words to a profound place in life. Chances are you need to grieve something right now. *Coram Deo* is about being there and not running. Those ancient words from King Solomon say it best.

Read them—and weep.

9

Sojourners

Have you ever scratched your head, wondering what was happening in your life? The journey definitely has its twists and turns. I always seem to forget that trying to control those twists and turns is almost always a dead end detour. There is a false hope that we can manage the path. The better view is to embrace the path, celebrating the peaks and mourning the valleys. Then we begin to realize that the travels of life are making us. We do not create the trip.

You've probably heard the story of a group of small animals that decided they needed a King. The first step was to make a list of attributes that a good King should have. Character traits such as patience, courage, decisive, compassionate, communication skills and wise. They decided to do some interviews; the process came up empty. Rather than dilute the criterion, they decided to send one from their group to the far reaches of the forest to find a candidate.

After drawing straws, the lot fell to Pocket Gopher. Because he didn't want to let the others down, he decided to strike out the very next morning. Pocket Gopher didn't sleep well that night, and the next morning left with a small pack and all the supplies he could carry.

His travels brought many encounters with several different animals. Many times he had to escape to save his own life. Other times he had to offer encouraging words to the down trodden. He made critical choices to escape injury and insult. At one point even risking his own neck to gather food for a nest of sparrows that were orphaned.

His adventures brought him to many interesting situations and in touch with many unique characters. He asked several if they had any interest in being a King. Each time, he was turned down.

Finally, discouraged and worn out, he gave up and traveled back to his friends with the bad news: there are no Kings out there.

His friends saw him coming and decided to throw a homecoming party. Of course they wanted to know all about the adventure and eventually as they were all gathered around, they wanted to know who their King was going to be. Pocket Gopher showed his travel slides and they began to get the picture. They watched as he escaped the cunning fox. They were inspired as he captured nourishment for the sparrows. They huddled together in fear as he explained the long cold nights and the strange forest sounds. They saw the rejection from all the animals who didn't want to be King.

Finally Blue Jay could stand it no longer and said, "I nominate Pocket Gopher to be our King. It's obvious that Pocket Gopher has demonstrated all the qualities we desire in a King. His adventures have revealed his true person."

In our secular, western way of thinking, we begin to believe that character can be learned from a book or a seminar. We educate ourselves in the ways of the journey, thinking that we will have something to offer the pilgrimage. This breeds self importance, pride, defensive walls in relationships and a cacophony in our lives that runs counter to our true identities.

We forget that it's the journey itself that has something to offer the sojourner.

Part of my journey is the business I've been given to manage and lead. We came to a crossroads in the formation of the small financial planning firm and needed a name. Several were kicked around. We landed on Compass Financial.

There are so many analogies to pull from a compass, your life journey and your financial stewardship. It's a rich, spacious name that I'm proud of to this day.

Compasses have four primary functions:

1. They allow you to maintain a straight line of travel by following a bearing.

2. They help orientation with a map to make landmark identification easier, such as a stream.

3. Thirdly, the compass marks your direction.

4. And, you can locate your position by taking several bearings and plotting them on a map.

In general, a compass can help you find your bearings when you are lost on a hike or long walk. Finding our bearings on the life pilgrimage can be more difficult. A compass will always have the four main directions on its face. Here are some North, South, East and West markers for your life's compass.

1. **Think Small.** Largeness is amplified in our culture. We buy in by thinking we have to be growing. Our net worth has to grow, our houses must get bigger, our span of power has to increase. Bigger is better. What a lie! Freedom and peace comes through contentment with small things. In a recent period of solitude, there were many hours quietly spent sitting, thinking, praying and listening. During those holy times, a certain bird was my frequent companion.

One of the points that I needed to hear was that Creation needed to play a deeper role in my journey. There is a calling and yearning I now have to be in the middle of Creation. The One managing and creating the journey of my life was giving me a significant clue, and I happened to be listening. I do wonder how many clues have passed by due to the noise and hustle of life. This one didn't and I have been restructuring the journey to include ample space for Creation.

These small inklings that connect with our heart usually won't come when we are on a stage or in the middle of a busy day. We will sense the ache for something more, but it's difficult to hear and know the message when we are enamored with big. The goal is to keep things small and simple.

2. **Think Quiet.** How many minutes during a day is there total quiet in your world? When there is noise we are being inundated with someone else's agenda intruding on our journey.

Talk radio is a good example. The hot topic of the day is interesting and the varied viewpoints make for good debate. At the end of the day, though, I'm more confused than ever on the controversial topic. This doesn't fit with someone who is in control of the journey. Controllers know. Obtaining more information isn't the answer; it only compounds the problem.

What I really need in this situation is a good two to five mile jog with no noise. These times of quiet have a way of purging and getting thoughts down to the core of the heart. Where there is noise, there is a high probability that we are losing some of our own voice, identity and purpose.

Those who are free have made time in quiet to know who they are. These individuals are very intimidating, and rarely do they have to make a strong case through debate to prove something. Quiet is better than noise. It is silence that gives our words shape and meaning. How does that quote go? "Better to be thought a fool than to speak and remove all doubt." I have much to learn in this area.

3. **Think Slow.** This is a tough sell in our culture. We are taught through technology to expect fast. Truth about the journey will not come to those who demand it on their terms. Learn to slow down. I was coached early in my sales career that one of the ways to project success is to walk faster, with purpose. Those little hints may work for a while, but eventually the house of cards will fall, collapsing under the weight of the hectic pace.

The business world is full of individuals wanting to throw out a perception of success. This perception is built on big, noise, and fast. We are taught to pursue, set goals and reach for the stars, as quickly as possible. When the journey throws a curve at us, it is viewed as an interruption and a distraction, instead of a message. The curves could actually be a space to work on the foundation of our lives that will reveal a deeper purpose.

Eventually our fast-paced culture leads us into an identity based on function and what we do. The journey is best lived out of an identity based on person, who we really are. Slowing down helps give a renewed perspective to our true identity.

4. **Think Companion.** Fellow sojourners can be an invaluable source of help in our travels. We really don't need someone to tell us more about our journey. We are equipped very nicely to interpret the path and look for meaning. What we

really need at times is someone to put their arm around us when we are afraid. Someone who will walk alongside.

It really helps if this person is ahead of us in his own personal adventure. He or she have usually learned that there are mysteries along the way and that it's better to enter the mystery in silence and awe. Companions like this is very rare, but very helpful. They don't take away lonely from our hearts, but they allow us space to be there and listen. Encouraging us when it is time to get up and move on, or prodding us to stop walking and sit to listen for a while.

Have you ever had someone like this in your life?

These words have been about *Coram Deo* with your journey. Being present and at peace with the human role of sojourner. We just weren't created to control the path, our place is to do the walking, with a good compass. God speed to you on the path.

Living Large is about living slow, quiet and simple. A spacious life is large enough to accept room for mystery, confusion, surprises and…wonder.

10

Grandma's Quilt

I never take a beautiful quilt for granted. I have come to appreciate the love in every stitch, and realize a quilt is not for staying warm but for providing a quiet comfort and a heritage beyond the years. Quilters are special artists. The pieces become the whole. I marvel at that.

Is it any wonder that a group of Iowa women felt compelled immediately after 9/11 to create hundreds of quilts to be given to the families of the victims? A very personal show of love and compassion for strangers in a very human way.

Grandma Pearson was a quilter. She loved to save all types of old clothing, curtains and other types of cloth. After cutting them into four-inch squares or six-inch squares, the material would go into a bag for the next project. Scraps with a future purpose.

The pieces of cloth would get sewn together creating the cover of the quilt. Alone, some of the pieces were downright ugly. Remember the lime green leisure suits of the 70's? But trained hands and a keen eye pulled the pieces together; the mixing of the various remnants became a work of art. In the end, it always looked like the fabrics were intended to be part of the quilt from the beginning.

Every square has a purpose and a place in the quilt. Relationships in life are this way. With some reflection and space we begin to know where a specific relationship goes into the quilt and fabric of our lives. What a surprise to find that the one square of ugly cloth looks really good in the whole scheme of things.

LOVE YOUR NEIGHBOR AS YOURSELF

We are caught in lonely times. The natural tendency is to place this loneliness at the feet of others. This carries expectations that we want them to fill the void. In reality there is internal heart work that we need to do to ourselves.

How do we learn to love ourselves? It sounds selfish and it's easy to think that selfish is bad. Selfish is good. Narcissism is bad; selfish is good. Narcissistic-addiction to self is a miserable state. The nurturing of self is healthy and gives us the foundation to really love another.

What about the instruction *"Do nothing out of selfish ambition, or vain conceit"* *[Phillipians 2:3]*—that is precisely the truth. For years I tried to put the longings and ache of my heart on others. Someone could surely ease the pain of the soul. This was selfish. In a place of pride, the only person that matters is "me" and I seek ways to use another person to boost my own soul. How foolish and small.

We can easily take expectations into relationships that are unfair. These expectations can easily set the relationship up for failure. The relationship becomes a performance-based dead end street. When performance becomes the measure of relationships, love dies.

It is unfair of me to expect my family or friends to meet the longings of my heart. Lonely is not something to put on top of a relationship. Doing my lonely work has to start with me. No one else. This is the ultimate act of denying self.

Until we befriend ourselves, we can't really befriend others.

When is the last time you nurtured your self? I'm calling for you to lavish care on your self. Will you accept the call? Those around you will immediately notice the change. You will turn into a lover, because you are learning to love and nurture yourself.

We have an incredibly rich model for this, the Trinity. Father, Son, Holy Ghost. Three in one, One in three. *Coram Deo.* They are present with each other; no separation.

Is it any wonder that we have mind, body and spirit? Will you allow all three to be present in your life? This is a place of health that brings us to holy ground in our lives. This place is intense with mystery, joy, sorrow, pain and hope.

Eventually we may be ready to venture out there and add some relationship squares to the quilt of our life. How do we love neighbor? Who is neighbor? Neighbor probably starts with spouse, children, parents, grandparents, uncles, aunts, etc. Time for a story—a familiar story.

> *There was once a man traveling from Jerusalem to Jericho. On the way, he was attacked by robbers. They took his clothes, beat him up and went off leaving him half dead. Luckily a priest was on his way down the same road, but when he saw him he angled across to the other side. Then a Levite religious man showed up; he also avoided the injured man.*

> *A Samaritan traveling the road came on him. When he saw the man's condition, his heart went out to him. He gave him first aid, disinfecting and bandaging his wounds. Then he lifted him onto his donkey, led him to an inn, and made him comfortable. In the morning he took out two silver coins and gave them to the innkeeper, saying "Take good care of him. If it costs any more, put it on my bill—I'll pay you on my way back."*

Which of the three acted like a neighbor? Go and do is the point of the story.

Defining who the neighbors are in my life is the wrong question. Going and doing is the proper activity.

There have been too many hours spent learning about love and too few going and doing.

What does going and doing look like? *Coram Deo*. Present with another. Words aren't necessary; expectations are gone. We have befriended self and are now ready to be with another. What a work of love! The quilt is finally ready.

I always knew Grandma loved me. The quilt she gave me was a reminder of the nurturing that happened as she quilted. There is time to nurture self, think, confess and release the cares of life with each new stitch. Perhaps we all ought to take up quilting. It's an opportunity to be with self, working with our hands and nurturing our souls. We were created to care for our mind, body and soul in a good way and it's not narcissism.

Go, care for your heart. Then you will really have something of beauty to offer another.

11

Conclusion

✦

Coram Deo reprise

○ ○

"Thanks for allowing me to come alongside you in this."

—*A Friend*

Wow! I have thought much about the statement. It's got to be one of the top five things someone has ever said to me. Let's parse it out a bit.

Thanks for allowing me... He recognized that he was there by privilege. He wasn't barging his way in. The implication is that he knew this was difficult territory in which we were heading and he was excited to be along for the ride.

To come alongside... He didn't want to rush in and start preaching—a top-down mentality. He wasn't intending to let me get by with lazy statements and actions, thereby running roughshod over the truth—a doormat mentality. He said alongside. Listening with an ear for truth. This requires *Coram Deo*. The face of God. The friend is present in his own life and it frees him to be present with others. To come alongside.

...you in this. We all have our moments. He didn't want to come in and control it or take over my whole life. He just wanted to participate in that space of time. I have had way too many friends over the years who prefer to watch from the stands. Shouting encouragement and heckling......but they have never come down on the field....alongside. Weeding these spectator friends out of our lives is a healthy thing.

48

"Alongsiders" are inspirational when they freely participate in our own lives. Listening and watching for the face of God. Seeing and hearing, we fall to our knees in awe and wonder at the holiness of the moment. At this moment, unbelief that this is happening to us and belief with no doubts that something very large is happening, courses through our souls simultaneously.

My wish for you is a sense of presence that invades your life.

Coram Deo

Big Mud Puddles and Sunny Yellow Dandelions

Author Unknown

When I look at a patch of dandelions, I see a bunch of weeds that are going to take over my yard.

My kids see flowers for Mom and blowing white fluff you can wish on.

When I look at an old drunk and he smiles at me, I see a smelly, dirty person who probably wants money and I look away.

My kids see someone smiling at them and they smile back.

When I hear music I love, I know I can't carry a tune and don't have much rhythm so I sit self-consciously and listen.

My kids feel the beat and move to it. They sing out the words. If they don't know them, they make up their own.

When I feel wind on my face, I brace myself against it. I feel it messing up my hair and pulling me back when I walk.

My kids close their eyes, spread their arms and fly with it, until they fall to the ground laughing.

When I pray, I say thee and thou and grant me this, give me that.

My kids say, "Hi God! Thanks for my toys and my friends. Please keep the bad dreams away tonight. Sorry, I don't want to go to Heaven yet. I would miss my Mommy and Daddy."

When I see a mud puddle I step around it. I see muddy shoes and dirty carpets.

My kids sit in it. They see dams to build, rivers to cross, and worms to play with.

I wonder if we are given kids to teach or to learn from? No wonder God loves the little children!

Enjoy the little things in life, for one day you may look back and realize they were the big things.

I wish you Big Mud Puddles and Sunny Yellow Dandelions!!!

Acknowledgements

I'd like to thank all those who are "present" with me in life, but especially......

My "partner in time" is the best. We journey together, listening with hope. The best is yet to come! Thanks Sandra.

Children are a gift from Above. I have learned more than I could ever teach you. Thanks Jonathan, Alicia, Caleb and Chelsea.

Thanks to the folks (Scott and Joyce) for the gift of life itself.

My partner in this project, Bob Coffman, kept me moving on this journey. Our conversations were a lesson in presence. I appreciate you coming alongside me in this endeavor.

Many thanks to all those who reviewed the copy of the text and offered ideas and suggestions; Nawal, Brenda, Dee, Tim, and Julie. Thanks for your time and insight.

About the Author

Kurt Pearson has learned the challenges of living on the balance beam of life, trying to accommodate a busy professional life while seeking a meaningful personal and family life. He knows he is not alone!

His perspectives have been shaped by quiet time spent in a tree stand deep in his wooded timber and refined by the quiet reflections allowed during a 50-minute cigar. He also enjoys the unconditional love and companionship of his chocolate Labrador, Hershey, who has heard it all.

Above all else, he has learned the value of seeking silence, solitude and inner peace.

Kurt is a Certified Financial Planner™ and founder of Compass Financial Services. But above all, he is a husband and father, and readily admits he has learned far more from his family than he has taught them.

In his professional role as counselor and advisor, he sees firsthand the life goals, dreams and struggles of those sitting across his desk. He hears what makes others anxious. He sees where they put their priorities. Watches their family grow and mature and become wise.

He knows there is no other choice than living a God-centered life, with spiritually-driven decisions and actions. Anything less results in a small and shallow life.

This book is not about the author, it is about you and the life choices your family makes in pursuit of not only a full life but a larger life—lived *Coram Deo.*

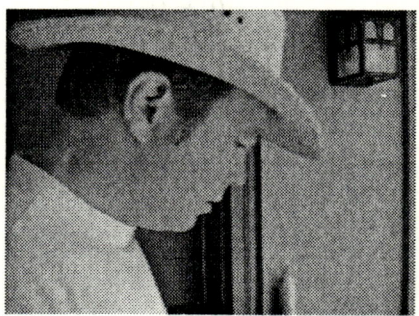

0-595-34834-3

Printed in the United States
27213LVS00005B/427-435

9 780595 348343